Love and Emotions

By

Yolanda P. Tyson

Copyright © 2022 Yolanda P. Tyson
ISBN: 979-8-9855817-7-5

All rights reserved. No part of this book may be reproduced or transmitted in any form or by any means, electronic or mechanical, including photocopying, recording, or by any information storage and retrieval system, without permission in writing from the copyright owner.

The views expressed in this work are solely those of the author and do not necessarily reflect the views of the publisher, and the publisher disclaims any responsibility for them.

Any people depicted in stock imagery provided by Getty Images are models, such images are being used for illustrative purposes only. Certain stock imagery © Getty Images.

To order additional copies of this book, contact:
1177 6th Ave 5th Floor
New York, NY 10036, USA
Phone: (+1 347-922-3779)
info@proislepublishing.com

Content

1. Celebrity Crush
2. In The Dark
3. Wrongfully Accused
4. Zodiac Love
5. Number Two King
6. Masked Man
7. Sweating
8. In Love Alone
9. I'm Beautiful
10. The Ugly Truth
11. Right & Wrong Way
12. Yumi
13. Just A Little More Jesus
14. Let It Go
15. In Love From A Distance
16. Real Love
17. Until Next Time
18. Loyalty
19. How Deep Is Your Love?
20. Put A Ring On It
21. Clueless Mom
22. It Happened
23. In The Mood
24. Falling In Love
25. I Love You, But I Don't Care
26. Why Me Baby?
27. When I Give My Love
28. Lather Up
29. Come Back
30. I'm Going For Mines
31. Miracles Happen
32. I'm Coming
33. Don't Believe Hear Say
34. Happy Mother's Day
35. It's Not That Serious
36. Happy Father's Day
37. The Right Choice
38. It Ain't Easy
39. I Want To Be Loved
40. A Closed Mouth
41. Could It Be?
42. It's You
43. Forever Mine
44. Depression Hurts
45. Tears Of Joy
46. Forbidden Love
47. Giving Thanks
48. My Husband
49. Reason For The Season
50. I'm Not Ready
51. Are We Over
52. Tell Me Now
53. The Search Is Over
54. My Mother
55. My Father
56. I Love You
57. It Was Never OK
58. Colors
59. Life Is Cold
60. No Exception

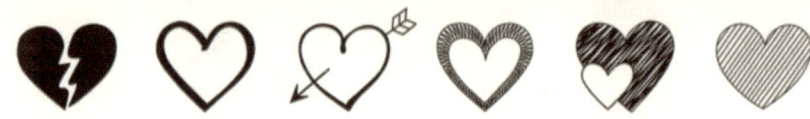

Celebrity Crush

My celebrity crush is a definite 100% real man, I want to try & get close to him any way I can. I wish he can come & get with me, if we do get together, anything goes. I'll do anything to feel just a touch of his hands from my lips to my hips, down to my toes.

I'm a chocolate girl & I want him to be part of my whole world. When I see him at concerts, I want to get up on it. I would never have him feeling like he's on a merry-go-round because I'll never let him down. I don't get caught up in rumours because I don't believe in he say/she say, as long as I get to satisfy you, there's nothing we can't do.

We won't stop, even if I make you sweat, I'll make sure it'll be a night we won't forget. Thinking about him got my mind twisted. We can go out in the rain, but it won't be for you to cry because I'll never cause you pain. I'll give all my love to you. I also don't mind some hood sex when we're together, I'll make sure nobody comes to interfere because we're going to make it last forever.

In The Dark

Tell me how you feel & please keep it real. I want to know what's on your mind. What have you been thinking about, instead of holding it inside, I want you to let it all out.

If I had something I needed to say, I won't hesitate & take all day. I'm not ashamed to talk & you shouldn't neither, if you won't talk to me, get on your knees & pray, you'll feel better either way.

Talk to me; I have no idea what's wrong with you. I have no clue what to do, why are you keeping secrets from me? After all we've been through, I want to know everything that's on your mind & in your heart, but whatever you do, please don't keep me in the dark.

Wrongfully Accused

Getting accused of something is never good, being wrongfully accused is the worst feeling & that really hurts especially when it ruins a good ongoing relationship.

You love that person so very much, you'll do just about anything to make them feel happiness, only to find out that the person couldn't care less, because as soon as something goes wrong, you're the blame with not a single evidence to back up their story, still you get punished, isn't that a shame?

I feel our whole relationship was just a game to you & I just got played. Finally you allow me to defend myself & see that I'm innocent, but yet my punishment still remains the same.

I could understand it better if I would have done something wrong, but that's not it at all. You just needed an excuse, you wanted to get rid of me all along.

Zodiac Love

I've been with my boyfriend for a very long time. Our relationship feels almost like a fairy tale, like it's a dream come true.

One night of being bored, I just looked up my sign & asked "if it was a compatible match with his?" I was shocked & speechless with everything I read, it was nothing else to be said.

So far it seems right, it also said "it's not impossible for us to fall in love & get married, hopefully we might, because we do love each other very much.

Everything is going so well, sometimes it's hard to believe that this could be really true, but as I compared our relationship to the stories I read, it speaks exactly about us. I'm absolutely sure of our relationship especially with our love & our trust.

Number Two King

My baby, my handsome king, I love you so much, you are my everything. I'm proud to be called your queen.

You are my friend, my lover, my soul mate, the reason why my heartbeat. You're my angel sent from the heaven above, to fill me with happiness, joy, & most of all, love.

All other men in this world, didn't give me half the smiles that you bring. I'm so used to always being let down; I have smiles just thinking of you when you're not around; you will always & forever be my number two king.

Don't be offended, for god is my number one king over all kings & I will always & forever love you my partner, lover, friend, soul mate, and my everything.
I'm so grateful to have you in my life & I'll be even more grateful when I become your wife.

Masked Man

We've been in a relationship for a few months now & we've gotten quite close, but talking on the phone, hanging out, & video chatting is what I would like most.

All we do is send pictures & text, how could you love me? Although you claim you do, if we don't have anymore communication, we're through.

I'm fed up with all of this texting. My hands & fingers are sore & unlike you, I can't take it anymore, especially over someone I never seen before, so either we communicate right or I'm not texting you another night

Sweating

I'm wondering if I can make this last forever because I'm playing for keeps & going for mine. Don't stop your love for me, no matter the weather. I'll have you sweating & calling my name, making you wish we were in the rain.

You'll see that there's nobody who can do you like me, I'll have you so twisted in love with me, you'd do a remix calling it "twisted in ecstasy".

Keep it coming, I love to sweat, especially when I get to grind on you. Let's go to bed, I'm ready for my test drive. You feel so good, I can't let you go, when we don't talk, I'm missing you like crazy.

I really love you, I want you to let me love you. I know all of the hurt & pain you've been through & I would never do that to you.

In Love Alone

I love you, why don't you love me too? I don't know why I still stay after all you put me through. No matter what I do, it's always wrong, never good enough for you, than I have to hear you complain all day & night long.

We've been together for too many years, I cook, go shopping, do your laundry & clean, but all you do is be mean, causing me to cry so many tears.

Well I can't take no more; whenever I come home, you're gone, when you do come home, no hug, kiss, not even a hello; I think it's about time to let you know, that if you don't change, I'm packing your things & we're going our separate ways, I deserve better days & I'm fed up with being in love alone.

I'm Beautiful

I'm beautiful, special, & unique in my own way. I get more beautiful loving myself more & more everyday. I'm beautiful; both inside & out, can't nobody tell me what I'm about.

I've got looks, breast, hips, thighs, ass, & most of all, I have class; because I don't dress like trash. I'm one of a kind, I think with my brain, not my behind.

Don't hate me because I'm me, you can never be me, because I'm me. I'm beautiful I don't need to wear makeup except lipstick & lip gloss, can't nobody tell me about me because I'm the boss.

I don't care about what you think about me. I'm proud of who I am. I'm beautiful whether you like it or not; I look in the mirror at least ten times a day & each time I smile loving what I see, my reflection looking back at me, but my beauty goes beyond of what the eyes may see.

The Ugly Truth

Baby; there's something we need to talk about; that I just found out, this is really hard for me, so please don't scream & shout.

This occurred before we had a chance to meet; I promise I did not cheat, after I'm done with what I need to say, please don't walk away; I'm loving you more everyday.

I don't want you to leave me, in your arms is where I want to be. Every thought of me hurting you makes me cry because it's hurting me more, I don't know why & I don't know exactly when, but baby please don't let it be the end, our future hasn't yet started to begin, there's so much for us to see & do, please just don't say "we're through".

Right & Wrong Way

"I'm young & I'm ready"; age 35 & I'm ready for my test drive. Fantasizing about you make me feel so alive.

You climbing on top of me; making me say ooh, you feel so good, I'm like a boomerang, I'm coming back to you, keep it coming, I want all of your good loving.

If something just ain't right, tell me what is it, show me, I'll give you whatcha like, whatever you want. I only want to please you, I'm way above 21, so we can have fun, one on one, it'll be a wonderful thing, no matter what we do.

Trust me, it gets better, come into my bedroom. I want to be all over your body; tell me it's me you want, I'm not ready for you to stop, but now it's my turn to be on top.

Yumi

After we ate dinner; now it's time for our dessert. First we take a hot shower, we stay in there for @ least an hour, causing the mirrors to fill up with steam, finally we get out & get the ice cream.

I put it on & we're eating it off each other's body, making each other feel so good, but we're not done; you go & get the honey, now it's time to get sticky, but here's where it gets tricky; I go & get the milk chocolate & caramel syrups for a more tasty treat, my how you taste so sweet.

Before we eat everything off of each other, I'm thinking we're about to make good love, I want to love you down; you put our loving through the test by topping off the rest, with some whipped cream, but it isn't as good as it may seem, I woke up realizing it was all just a yumi dream.

Just A Little More Jesus

I have faith, I believe in Jesus Christ. I know he died for my sins & through him; I know I'm forgiven & I'm saved, although I've been through a lot, I try to be brave.

Every now & than I pray, I often cry almost everyday, because of what I been through in the past. Sometimes I have negative thoughts, hopefully they won't last.

I don't act on those thoughts because I know they can get me into a lot of trouble; I wish I can get these thoughts out of my head, so to avoid it, I'll leave it in Jesus hands instead.

Just because I'm saved don't make me complete; I still need just a little more Jesus to stand on my own two feet.

Let It Go

I want to be free from all of my past burdens. I have forgave, I've been forgiven, but there's one thing that stays on my mind, because the devil won't let me leave it behind.

It happened, I know the truth & Jesus does too, he knows everything that I've been through.

I know I should "let go & let god", but it isn't easy knowing what I feel inside. I wish I could just sit these feelings aside.

Nobody believed me when I told, but knowing what I do know, it's true, so how can I keep a heart of gold?

Deep inside, I really want to let it go, I'm fed up with crying everyday, I will somehow, some way, let it go one day.

In Love From A Distance

I love you, you love me, I can't wait until we can be together as a family should be.

Texting & sending pictures isn't enough, we have to admit long distant relationships are tough, but you're worth the wait, when we reunite everything will be great. It's unexplainable, hard to believe, but it's true, you are my soul mate.

Nobody can make me feel the way you do. Imagining the smile on your face, tells me that our love can never be replaced.

Sometimes it seems our relationship is too good to be true, but we're going to be together, no matter what we go through; the good times & the bad, whether we're happy or sad.

Whenever we talk makes me feel good. I'm looking forward to be reunited, so you can make me feel the way a woman should. In each other's arms is where we belong, your lips, kissing me on mine, feeling your touch would be so fine.

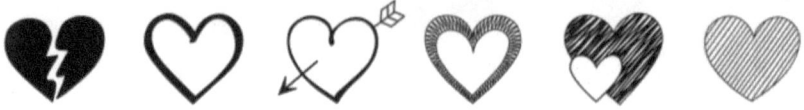

Real Love

Real love isn't just loving someone when it's convenient for you; it's loving each other no matter what you go through.

Love isn't based on money, sex, whether you live near or far, nor if one of you is a nerd & the other's a star.

It's feeling the chills you get through your body & smiles just thinking of that special someone with the love growing stronger everyday; even if you're both a long distance away.

It's loving each other unconditionally regardless about the thoughts of friends & family & you are willing to do anything to keep each other happy.

Until Next Time

Today is the day, we say our final goodbye. It's about time for us to have a new beginning & a fresh start; in order for me to do that I have to follow my heart; go to a different location that's not too far away, but we can't stay.

Saying goodbye doesn't have to mean forever. We can write each other & sometimes visit; again we'll be together, there are too many bad memories that's stuck in my mind & this is the only conclusion I came up with to leave them behind.

It's very difficult for me, as it is for you, but there is too much to handle after all that I've been through, so that's why I have to go away, we'll see each other again someday & don't worry I have Jesus to guide me along the way.

Loyalty

People asked "how can I stay loyal in a long distant relationship? Why don't I cheat?" the answer is simple "I love him". I wouldn't want him to cheat & be unfaithful to me, so whether we're near or far, I'm going to be the best I could be for him & our new family.

There are times when I get in the mood, but I don't cheat; that's just being cruel; I put on some music, take a long hot shower while fantasizing about us being together.

He's always on my mind & forever in my heart. My love for him is so strong, I wouldn't cheat on him if I had the opportunity to be with someone else. I wouldn't betray our love & I would never forgive myself.

How Deep Is Your Love?

How deep is your love for me? Do you really love me as much as I love you; after all we've been through?

I'll do just about anything to make you happy, that's a fact & you know that, but would you be willing to do the same for me?

I want us to get married & extend our family, but do you feel the same way? Because I think about it everyday. There's not a day that goes by that I don't have you in my heart & on my mind.

You are my soul mate, we were meant to be together forever, but I noticed you barely take interest in anything I like to do, are you even interested in me @ all?

Why can't I seem to make you happy? I love you so much, it's almost hard to describe, but I need to know & hear from you; how deep is your love for me?

Put A Ring On It

I'm already ready, when you are. I'm always going to love you, whether we live near or far. You have my whole heart, mind, & body belongs to you. I want to have our dreams come true.

For us to live happily ever after; when you hold me in your arms, I want to be held close & tight. I know you love me, you tell me everyday & show me in a unique way, but before we go any further, we need to make it official & do it right.

For the sake of our love for each other & our family, let's do it the right way. I'd love to wake up to you everyday. If you really want me to be in your life; why not make me your wife? My left hand is waiting, so put a ring on it.

Clueless Mom

A young woman who has just given birth; little that she know the doctor lied & told her that her baby died, placing a stillborn in her arms.

Later selling the young woman's baby to be adopted by another young lady. Other's whom were involved are now feeling a lot of guilt, they confronted the doctor of his shameful wrong doing. He says "he did it so his daughter won't get killed".

I almost feel bad for the young woman that doesn't know her baby is still alive & doing well; she met the baby & fell in love @ the same time accepts the baby as her niece; she feels so good & complete when she's around especially when she holds her, if she only knew it was her baby she would have some peace.

People thinks she's getting too attached & needs space, not knowing the baby she holds is her very own looking back @ her face.

It Happened

I told the truth; how could she not believe me? Although it happened years ago, I still remember it like it was yesterday.

He inappropriately touched me, for her to tell me "it was just a dream" seemed too extreme. I asked myself "how can he do this to his own niece?" nobody believed me but for the sake of his new addition to his family, I didn't call the police.

As the years went by; everytime I remember this night, I just sit alone & cry without telling anyone else the reason why & just because she doesn't believe me makes it right.

In The Mood

Tonight is the night everything is gonna be alright. I want you; can it be, that I know you want me too? Can we make love? How do you like it? Come with me, than you'll see that we were meant to be.

Don't have me all horny, I only want to please you. I'm a real woman, so I need a real man. Tell me, it's me you want. When I give my love, you can have whatever you want.

So put it on & put your loving through the test. Show me what you got & I'll show you where to hit the right spot. I can go all night; I'm giving you an open invitation to get in & out for us to have one on one time.

I always go after what I want, right now, I want you so I'm going for mines. I don't want to do wrong tonight, I want everything just right.

Falling In Love

Some people fall in love, than don't know what to do. I went looking for my man no matter what I had to go through; so he'll know that how I feel is real & that he would feel the same way about me too. You'll never get tired of hearing each other say "I love you".

Falling in love is a great feeling especially when that person loves you too & while thinking about that person your mind wanders off track & when times get rough you'll have each other's back.

But the greatest love of all is falling in love with Jesus Christ, that's one relationship that would never fail even if you end up in jail. His love will never stop, Jesus Christ, the king over all kings, he loves you throughout everything. He heals our hearts & save our souls, he's even there when nights are cold, Jesus love never gets old.

I Love You, But I Don't Care

I hate the fact that I feel this way & I feel like this everyday. I love you because you're family, but I don't care because of what you have done to me.
Not believing me when I told you, your son touched me inappropriately.

You had me arrested because you got hurt involving yourself in a fight that had nothing to do with you.

You called your other son to toss me out of the house like a trash bag because you wanted more money, which I couldn't afford, I gave you what I could spare & that was enough, too bad it wasn't enough for you because you don't care.

All of your children are grown & I have a child of my own, I struggle & have very little help, so I can support my little family. Not believing me when I told you I was touched inappropriately, accusing me of stealing; I love you because you're family, but expecting me to care is asking too much.

Why Me Baby?

I love you unconditionally, gave you all I had, how could you do this to me, to us, to your own family?

All the signs were there, how come I haven't seen them before? I was too deep in love to see, the whole while I'm being faithful & loyal to you, you wasn't loving me.

You're acting as if everything was fine, but you weren't really mine. I knew you were cheating, I didn't have the proof, now that I see for myself, I now know the truth.

You never did care, when we travelled everywhere, together near & far, no matter what I have given you, you always wanted more, but I gave it to you not knowing you were in this relationship with only one foot in the door.

When I Give My Love

When I give my love to you,
I promise I'm the only one you want to give yours to because I'm yours & you're forever mine.

Don't stop your love for me,
We love each other as anyone could see, I was meant for you & you for me.

When I give my love to you,
Please don't take advantage & abuse my love? It's one of a kind & unique, I will make your life complete you can never find another woman who can love you like me.

I'm the one you want
I'm the only one you need.
In each other's arms is where we should be, when I give my love to you, keep it & treasure as if it's your trophy.

Lather Up

In a hot shower, while the water runs down my body, feels so good. I grab the sponge to put soap on it, rubbing the sponge all over my body, the soap is lathering & dripping everywhere, than I stop to wash my hair.

Just when I thought I was done, I started fantasizing about how many ways I want to love you down with good love than you pull back the curtain & step inside, holding a sponge, we wash each other's body, making each other soapy, than we rinse while sharing a long passionate kiss, than the water gets cold & snaps me back into reality that you're really not here with me.

Come Back

I miss you so much, lying down with you @ night, waking up to you next to me, I miss that part of my life.

Going places, doing things together, what happened to our life that was supposed to last forever?

Thinking about you all day &night long, wondering "what did I do so wrong?" come back to our family. Here's where you belong, so please come back & make this house our home.

The sunshine has gone away, now only clouds drift by me everyday. I cry every night. Holding my pillow tight, wishing it was you, I still can't believe we're through.

You said "you'll love me forever" & I said the same to you, please come back, so the sun can shine again, this time we won't let it end.

Never again will we be together, because you don't love me anymore, so much for making it last forever, now I know you'll never come back.

I'm Going For Mines

For many years, I've had a huge crush & I feel it's about time, he knew about my feelings that I feel for him are real & true. Some people think I'm crazy to search for my handsome, sexy, baby, others feel that it's a waste of time because I'll never find him. Deep in my heart, he was already mines from the start & when we get together, I'm going to make sure nothing or nobody tear us apart.

Aside from being a huge fan, I want him to be my man. I also fantasize when I listen to his music, the lyrics makes me wish I was closer to him, he sings about how he's been betrayed in so many ways, he had a lot of good & bad days, he's just a man with a broken heart, well I want to be the one to put those pieces back together & love him forever.

Miracles Happen

Loved ones getting hit by a drunk driver everyday in such a tragic way "there's nothing else we can do" they say, but as a family, we came together to pray. She's gonna make it through because she's a survivor & it's another doctor that says "he knows what to do". Others say "it's impossible, she's badly damaged, bandaged from feet to head, pretty soon she'll be dead." the family didn't believe them, they believed in Dr. Jesus Christ instead.

Day after day, they waited & prayed, than they all got a surprise because later that day she opened her eyes. "he did it again!!!!" the family shouted. She pulled through because Dr. Jesus knew what to do. The bandages came off & her wounds healed. The doctors kept her one more day for observation, than she went to a different location, home where she belonged. Dr. Jesus mission have been complete, especially when she stood on her own two feet.

I'm Coming

We live so far apart, but we keep one another in each other's heart, for many years, I've been afraid to get on an airplane, well it's about time I face my fears & swallow my pride, pushing all of my fears aside, because I'm coming & don't mind @ all if it starts to rain, if I don't get close to you soon I'm going to go insane.

I'm traveling across this great blue sky, so I can be with my guy. I know I'll be leaving a lot of family & friends behind, but the way they treat me, I know they won't mind.

It's true, I'm coming from a different state to be with my soul mate, I just hope I don't arrive too late, even if I do, it'll be worth the wait, don't worry about me, I'll be there very soon you'll see, I'm coming so we can live happily.

Don't Believe Hear Say

I almost ruined a good relationship by listening to hear say. My feelings were hurt. When I confronted my man about the issue, what I had to say really hurt his feelings too.

We both cried while saying goodbye, but that didn't last for long, when I calmed down, I apologized after explaining everything, we gave our love another try after finding out, the hear say was just a big lie.

I tried to erase him out of my life, but I couldn't imagine being without him. I love him too much to let go. I had to tell him what was real, nothing or nobody will ever stop us from becoming husband & wife.

Never again will I allow hear say to get in the way. We were saying "I love you" to each other the next day.

Happy Mother's Day

A special day for your mother because you have no other. She brought you into this world, she didn't have to, but she did & for her to carry you in her belly for nine months or more, than give birth, you must been a very special kid; on this day, show her how much she's worth.

There are different types of mothers, adopted mothers, foster mothers, grandmothers, great grandmothers, god mothers, even surrogate mothers, but they all have one kind of love, unconditional.

Some mothers show their love in different ways (abusive) especially when they're not having one of their best days. Some kids get out of control, but no matter what, they can't get rid of mother's tight hold. She keeps you warm when it gets cold, so show her some love before she gets too old.

It's Not That Serious

Some things that belong to me, I keep very closely, I just don't allow anyone to handle my things without me being available to make sure not to be played for a fool.

It's not that serious for you to take it personally. I feel that way towards everybody, not just you. Wanting to end our friendship over something that belongs to me?

What a penalty, to end our friendship over something that's not that serious.

You talk about the things you did for me, I was there for you too. It's not that serious to throw our friendship down the drain that's just insane, but if that's what you want to do it's up to you.

Happy Father's Day

We're always celebrating the mothers, but what about the fathers? They're special too, without them there would be no children. Although fathers don't expect to be showered with flowers, candy, & gifts, there's nothing wrong with showing them love.

They help us with the children, especially with the boys in ways we mothers don't understand, they teach boys how to become a man.

When we're raising the children by ourselves, we do our best, but when the father's around, they handle the rest. Let's not forget about being a single dad, including the one with girls can be stressful & bad when they're in a certain mood, dad thinks it's an attitude, but he don't understand & becomes rude, some dads are used to being both dad & mom, be good to him while there's still time, & also it's not easy being a single mom while playing the part of the father also, so to all single moms, happy father's day to you too.

The Right Choice

The day I first saw your face, I wanted you in my space. The first few weeks we talked & I was playing hard to get. The feelings I had while in your arms, I shall never forget. When we're not together, I think about you all of the time.

Every thought of you makes me feel jitters down my spine. Everytime I kiss your lips. I feel passion through my body, from my fingertips down to my hips.

Each time I talk about us, it sounds like a fairy tale from a story book, as anyone could see, I was meant for you & you are meant for me. In love is where we were made to be. If you promise we'll always be together, I'll promise to love you forever.

It Ain't Easy

I don't get enough money, just a little bit to get by, sometimes that's not enough, not being able to work is tough.

I'm on a fixed income, sometimes I wonder, when will I be able to spend some?

I have a child who depends on me, sometimes I can't depend on myself, because I don't have enough money.

I have plans to save money, but when I have the chance, I always have to do something new.

I cry @ night because I don't feel right, not only I can't take care of me, but I can't take care of my family & it hurts that nobody wants to help me, help myself succeed.

I Want To Be Loved

Why don't you love me, I love you? My love for you is real, unconditional & true. I'll always love you no matter what we go through. When we shared our first kiss, I knew it was right. I think about you everyday & night. I miss you so much whenever you're out of my sight.

I'm so happy with you in my life, I was hoping someday to be your wife, but now I see it'll never come true, because you don't feel about me the way I feel about you.

I wanted our relationship to develop into something more & lasts for years instead everyday I cry tears. My feelings for you is hard to hide inside, can you blame me for wanting you by my side?

I love you so much, but I need more than your sexual touch. You have my whole heart & nobody else do, you know I'm willing to do any & everything for you, but on one condition, you have to love me too.

A Closed Mouth

It has always been said "a closed mouth won't get fed", that quote is so true. If you love someone, you should tell them how you feel & keep it real.

Some people hold in their feelings for a very long time, but when they finally found the courage to say anything, it'll be too late, than you start to feel bad because you lost the most important person in your life you ever had.

I told my crush how I felt, I couldn't keep my mouth closed, it feels great knowing that he knows, pretty soon everyone will too, know that he's no longer my crush, he's my man, & he's the only one I want to put a ring on my hand.

Could It Be?

Could it be, I finally met the man whom is right for me? My empty cup is now filling up, after all these years, I can now stop crying so many tears.

For many years, I've been rejected, it happened so much I now expect it, but often I walk away before I start to feel neglected, for once in a relationship I'd finally get respected.

This is too good to be true, I'd have to stay in this relationship longer to see if it will grow stronger.

His kiss, I can't resist, when I'm cold, he squeezes me in a tight hold. When we're together, he makes me feel good, just as a woman should. I wish I can be held like this forever.

It's You

It's you, the one whom have been in my thoughts & dreams, I guess being with you won't be so bad as it may seem.

It's you, the one I want to be with for life, maybe someday I'll be your wife.

It's you, whom I supposed to be with to keep our family together; hoping our love will last forever.

I love to see your smile & the glare in your eyes, everytime I see you, it's always a surprise.

It's you, I think of every night, wanting you next to me, holding each other tight.

It's you, whom always in my heart, the one I always loved right from the start.

Forever Mine

We've been together for many years, there were many times I cried, but you wiped away all of my tears, you gave me comfort throughout all my fears.

During the time of struggle, you were there on the double, you stood by my side when I was in trouble.

When I was homeless, lying around, you took my hand & pulled me up from the ground. You brought me to your home & said "here is where I belong & here is where I'll stay, so we'll be together everyday".

Today we got married, soon to be working on our family. I belong to you, you belong to me, I'm forever yours & you're forever mine.

Depression Hurts

Depression is like a rollercoaster ride, your emotions goes up & down, your head spins round & round, you'll never know what you'll feel inside.

Depression, it can either make you or break you, sometimes you don't know what to do, it can also make you feel like you're alone, as if all of your hopes & dreams are gone.

Depression can also cause you to isolate & rarely decide to participate. Most people say "that only medication can take it away".

This isn't true, medications can only make it adjusted & most medications can't be trusted. Many people deal with depression everyday, not only depression effects you; but it can have a great impact on your family & friends too.

Tears Of Joy

Today was the first time I had this experience. I have never felt this way before, as I was in deep thought while sitting on the floor, as usual when I'm thinking of him, it always puts a smile on my face, but today that wasn't the case.

I thought about all of the conversations we had, some were good & some were bad, but the way we can talk to each other about anything, sharing feelings & emotions without any arguments, just shows how well we communicate, he's definitely my soul mate, as I sat & thought I started to cry, so I told him how I feel, & with his response, I know our love for each other is for real.

Forbidden Love

Two different people whom love each other very much. Their love grows more rapidly with just a single touch. Many people don't want them as a couple because of their age range, but won't nothing change; still they're both adults, so their age shouldn't matter.

I don't see the big deal, who are they to say what you feel isn't real? Kissing you makes my toes curl, I don't care why people don't want me to be your girl. I'm your woman, you're my man, we're always going to be together, that's what people have to understand.

Giving Thanks

God is so good to us all; we shall give praise to him always; not only when we fall, give thanks unto the **Lord** for he is always on call.

Creator of all things, king over all kings, I thank you for everything, including the blessings you always bring.

To the **Lord God**, most high; the messiah, if I had a million tongues, I still can't thank you enough, for my miracle son Jeremiah.

Thank you **Lord**; for guiding me in the right path when I lost my way. Thank you **Lord** for saving me when I didn't think I was worthy to live another day.

When I thought all hope is gone; thank you **Lord** for showing me that as long as I have you, I am never alone.

My Husband

A man whom loves me unconditionally, & not care what anyone has to say, just keep me smiling all day.

A man whom is understanding, kind, gentle, keeps his hands to himself & don't fall in love with anyone else.

A man whom accepts & love my kids as his own; just as he loves me, so we'll be a family.

A man whom is honest, always tells the truth & never insecure about the friends I have next door.

A man whom stays out of trouble, whenever needed he'd be there on the double. If things on his mind, he's willing to sit down & talk, other than arguing & get up to walk away from the family we made together, because our love will last forever.

A man whom is willing to help me as much as he can, is what I expect from my husband.

Reason For The Season

Christ

Holy

Righteous

Itinerary

Saviour

Teacher

Messiah

Awesome

Salvation

I can't speak for all, but he is always there to catch me when I fall. When I was in trouble, he's always there on the double even throughout my struggle. As I was sick, almost near death, he saved me from taking my last breath.

During the time when I was depressed, lost & confused because I was abused, he helped me find my way & I'm being blessed everyday.

I'm so grateful you have your angels watching over me & protecting my family as we sleep through the night & are blessed to see the morning sunlight.

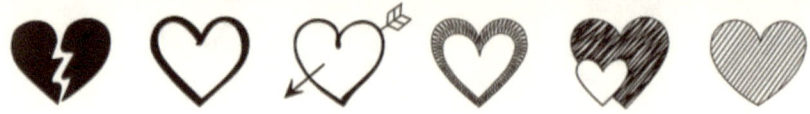

I'm Not Ready

All of this time we've been together, we didn't make it official, but we did promise to love each other forever.

We had our ups & downs, but that doesn't mean I don't want you around. I want you to stay, I'm not ready for you to walk away.

After all we've been through, you want me to pretend that I don't love you, just another day to have you by my side, can't express all of the emotions I feel inside. I love you too much & I'm not ready to say goodbye.

Are We Over?

Why do you doubt my love for you? I love you so much; more than anything in the world. I'll do anything for you as long as I continue to be your girl.

You are every girl's dream, but you made things bigger than it seem. You really broke my heart, when you tore our family apart.

We made a commitment that we would keep a bond that would hold us together forever, now it's broken & we haven't spoken.

All I wanted was to become your wife, but you kicked me out of your life. In your arms is where I want to be, but you no longer want to be with me.

I'm crying everyday, wanting you to bring your heart back to me, so we can be together as a family. I cry myself to sleep @ night, tears rolling down my cheeks while holding my pillow tight. I need to know, are we over?

Tell Me Now

If you love me, show me, tell me now, don't wait until I'm lying on my death bed, tell me while I'm still here on earth instead.

It doesn't matter if we haven't talked for months or even years, don't wait until my funeral to feel sad crying tears.

If you love me, let me know, so we can have a relationship & make it grow.

We're supposed to be a family, sharing different roots, but still from the same tree, so don't be afraid to show me, tell me now, don't wait until I'm in the ground.

The Search Is Over

The queen finally found her number two king. They both had their hearts broken before, now they don't have to hurt anymore.

When she found him, she expressed her love, he listened, opened his heart to her, now they love each other & will always be together.

Their love grows stronger each day, nothing or nobody will ever stand in their way. They will always be happy & their love will last forever.

No more let downs, broken hearts, & definitely no more tears. The search for love is now over, their kingdom is now complete, they have the whole world @ their feet. With the love of god & each other, they can't be beat.

My Mother

Our relationship could be better, so many ups & downs, so many times I tried to turn that around. We just can't get along & when we do, it don't last very long. It feels like us being mother & daughter is very wrong.

There was a time when I tried to buy her love, because I don't feel loved by her. I bought her gifts & treated her to different concerts, she never appreciated it. Nothing seems to work so I gave up. I appreciate the little things that she do for me, when she "helps" than I have to pay her back as if I owe her. I'm her only daughter, single mom, can't work, disability check isn't enough, no child support, so I'm struggling to get by, isn't she supposed to help me? Once in a while she does something from the heart.

I need that person to stick around, there's so much to talk about, so many feelings & emotions I need to let out, knowing her she won't believe me, when I tried talking to her, all she want to do is argue or brush it off like I don't matter, I guess I can never be heard. Now she says "she loves me", but I don't take it seriously because "actions speak louder than words", than she said "she rather help a bum on the street than to help me". Most of her words hurt especially coming from my own mother. I only get one, it feels bad that I don't fully love & trust her.

My Father

My father wasn't always here. There were times when I thought he didn't even care, just vanished out of thin air, nobody could find him anywhere. As I grew up I understood why he left, dealing with my mother made him stressed, he should have gotten a divorce first instead of cheating though.

When he came back, he wasn't fully on track. It seemed like every word spoken was lies, even promises were broken. He eventually got his priorities in order. I forgive him for all he has & hasn't done because nobody is perfect except god. I'm glad to have my dad by my side.

When other family claimed I was homeless (which I wasn't), called dhs & they wanted to take my son away, but my dad took us into his home for us to have another place to stay. I think about him often whenever we're apart, he'll always have my heart.

My dad is one of the best friends I ever had. When I'm feeling down, I can call him anytime, tell him how I feel & he always keep it real. I get excited & enjoy him, whenever he comes around, I enjoy the time we spend together, I'll always love my dad forever.

I Love You

I love you so much more than anything in this world, if you only knew the feelings I have for you. When you touch me, my heart pounds, I melt @ the way your voice sounds. I wish i could be your girl. I'll call you without having anything to say, just to hear you talk all day.

If only you knew how much I love you, I want you to love me too, than you'll see we were meant to be.

I know in the past, you have had relationships that didn't last, you always ended up with the broken heart, but I've loved you from the start, so I've come to put those broken pieces back together & our love, we'll make it last forever

It Was Never OK

How dare you think it was ok, for me to be treated that way? I considered you family, but you allowed someone much older to take advantage of me, you should have been bolder.

I wasn't even legal nor able to concert, how could you possibly assume that it would be ok? I would never allow anyone to do that to you, if you only knew how much pain that one night put me through.

I often cry about that night because you betrayed me, it isn't right & it's hard to explain to my family.
I pray that god have mercy on your souls, especially the man involved, he was old enough to be my dad. You should feel shame making me the blame, I feel so sad that I lost the closeness bond I ever had.

Colors

Don't judge me because of the color of my skin nor my race. Does it matter that we don't have the same face? We're all human, we bleed red blood.

We don't always have the same eye color, but the same vision that makes us able to see. You don't have to be my brother, for us to love one another.

Why do you care about my hair, the brand & colors of clothes I wear? I wear my clothes as I see fit, so your opinion isn't even worth it.

The violence need to stop, we're all different, but equally the same. Too much violence & hatred, only because of color is a shame.

Life Is Cold

Life is cold, when you have nobody to hold until you get old. Life is cold, after you done cooking, you sit down to eat while looking @ the empty seat. Life is cold, when you're sick & there's nobody there to rub their fingers through your hair & make sure you heal quick.

Life is cold when there's nobody around to make you smile when feeling depressed or stressed to lift your spirits off the ground. Life is cold, when you don't have anyone to give you the first kiss in the morning sunlight neither the last kiss good night. Life is cold, when your house is not a home because there's nobody there to call your own.

No Exception

Everyone knows the saying "keep your friends close & your enemies closer", well I think this saying applies to family too, so watch what you say & who you say it to because what you think is a secret, will eventually be thrown back against you.

They have some nerve to come into your house, eat up your food, laugh in your face, than gossip to you about other people when it isn't there place.

Don't be blindsided because they're family & you love them, if they can gossip about other people to you; you better believe they're talking about you too, just because you have a good connection, doesn't make you an exception.

www.ingramcontent.com/pod-product-compliance
Lightning Source LLC
LaVergne TN
LVHW041550070526
838199LV00046B/1893